Cambridge
Early Years

Mathematics

Learner's Book 3A

Alison Borthwick & Cherri Moseley

Contents

Note to parents and practitioners

This Learner's Book provides activities to support the first term of Maths for Cambridge Early Years 3.

Activities can be used at school or at home. Children will need support from an adult. Additional guidance about activities can be found in the **For practitioners** boxes.

Children will encounter the following characters within this book. You could ask children to point to the characters when they see them on the pages, and say their names.

The Learner's Book activities support the Teaching Resource activities. The Teaching Resource provides step-by-step coverage of the Cambridge Early Years curriculum and guidance on how the Learner's Book activities develop the curriculum learning statements.

Find 11

Colour and say.

Colour in number 11.

For practitioners

Count along the washing line with children if support is required. For additional challenge, ask *Colour in the number that is 1 less than 8. Colour in the number that is 2 more than 10. Which number is 5 less than 5? Which number is 11 less than 11? What do you notice?*

Find 15

Colour and say.

Colour in number 15.

For practitioners

Count along the caterpillar with children if support is required. For additional challenge, ask *Colour in the number that is 1 less than 18. Colour in the number that is 2 more than 11. Which number is 3 less than 13? Which number is 6 less than 16? What do you notice?*

How many dumplings on each plate?

Count and write.

Plate 1

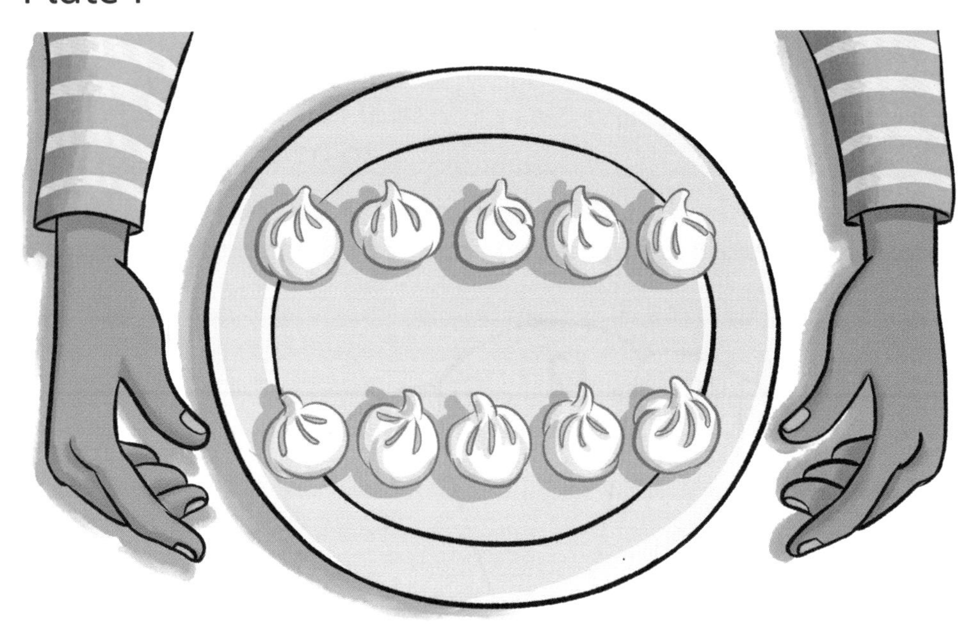

Cross out each dumpling as you count it.

Plate 2

For practitioners

Children count the number of dumplings on plate 1 and write the answer. Do the same for plate 2. Children should recognise that the number remains the same even when the objects are rearranged. Challenge children to arrange 10 (modelling clay) dumplings in different ways.

How many?

Count and match.

How many?

Count and colour.

Count the flowers. Colour the matching number.

Estimate how many

Estimate and circle.

Estimate the number of fruits in each picture.
Circle the numbers.

2 6 15

5 10 18

3 10 15

4 8 12

For practitioners

Children estimate the number of fruits rather than counting. An estimate does not need to be the actual number. Children are beginning to understand the general size of quantities.

How many in the jar?

Estimate and match.

3 6 10 16 20

For practitioners

Children estimate the number of fruits in each jar and then draw lines to match the jars to the numbers. An estimate does not need to be the actual number. Children are beginning to understand the general size of quantities.

Help Teddy find his gift box

Estimate and match.

Teddy is looking for the box containing 6 toys.
Draw a line to the right box.

For practitioners

Children estimate which box contains 6 toys and then draw a line from Teddy to the box. Children should reason, rather than count.

Counting on

Draw, count and circle.

Rabbit has 6 carrots. Draw I more carrot.

How many carrots does Rabbit have now?
Circle the number.

I 2 3 4 5 6 7 8 9 I0

Ten frames

Count and colour.

Colour to show 3 paint marks on the second ten frame. Circle the total number.

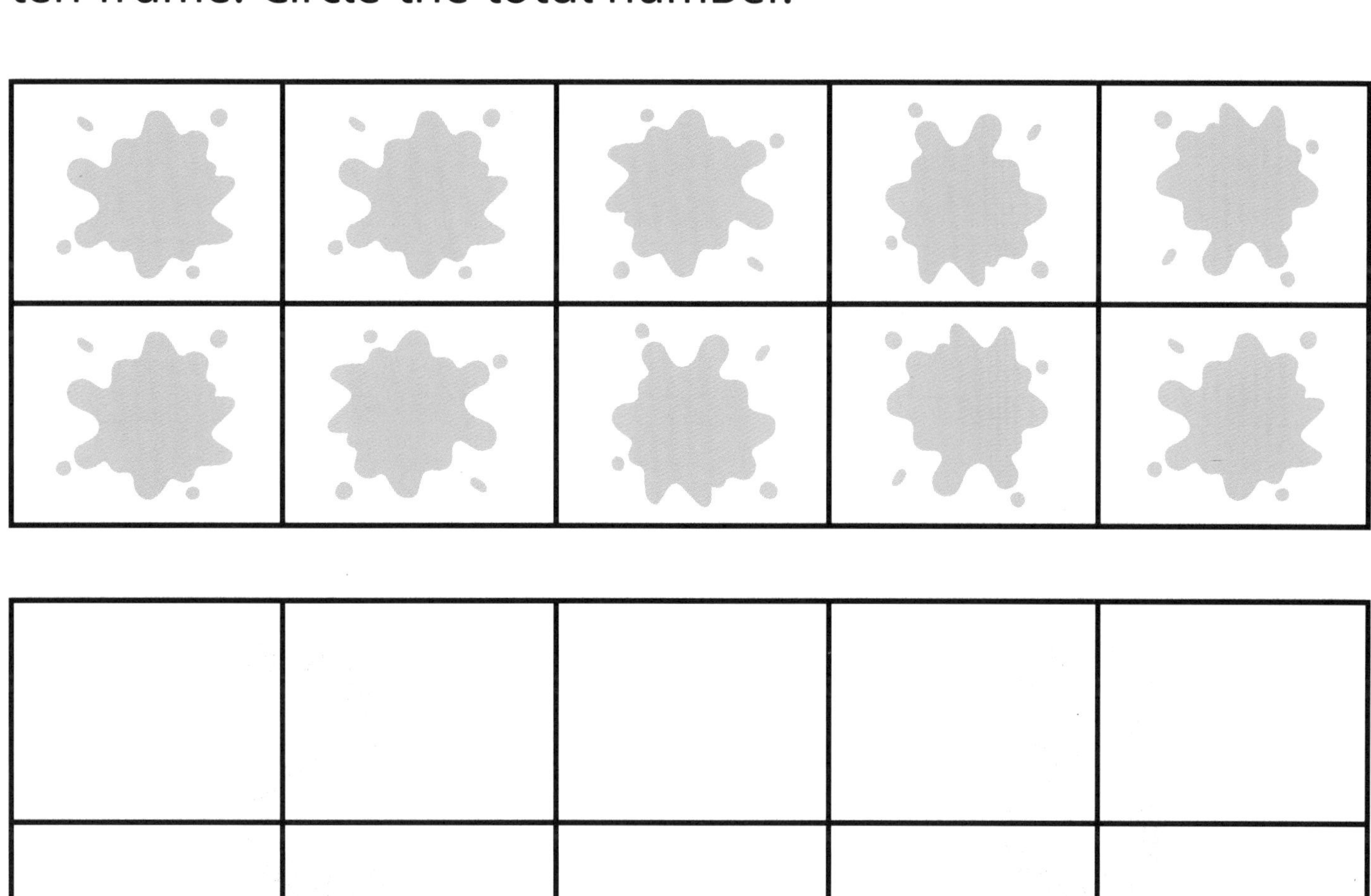

10 11 12 13 14 15 16 17 18 19 20

For practitioners

Children draw and colour to show 3 on the second ten frame. Encourage children to count on from 10 to find out how many paint marks there are altogether and circle the matching number.

How many altogether?

Work out.

Count on to find out how many pencils altogether.
Circle the number.

1 2 3 4 5 6 7 8 9 10 11 12 13 14 15 16 17 18 19 20

For practitioners

Children work out how many pencils there are altogether. Encourage them to use one of the numbers on the pot and count on the number on the other pot, instead of counting all the pencils. Challenge children to set up similar situations using different objects (e.g., balls).

Find the difference

Work out.

Work out the difference between the number of cars and aeroplanes. Circle the number.

1 2 3 4 5

For practitioners

Children work out the difference between the 2 rows of objects and then circle that number.

Counting back

Count and colour.

Frog jumps back by 2.
Colour the lily pad he lands on.

For practitioners

Check that children are counting jumps, and not counting the lily pad the frog is starting on. Encourage children to count back from the number the frog started on, e.g., the frog is sitting on 7, counting back 2, children will say 6, then 5. The frog is now on 5.

Subtraction

Use the number track to help you find your answer.

Circle.

Circle the answers on the number track.

What is 8 subtract 2?

1	2	3	4	5	6	7	8	9	10

Start at 4, count back 3.

1	2	3	4	5	6	7	8	9	10

Find the difference between 2 and 5.

1	2	3	4	5	6	7	8	9	10

For practitioners

Check that children understand what the question is asking of them.

Comparing lengths

Colour and tick.

Colour the longest pencil. Tick the shortest pencil.

Colour the tallest plant. Tick the shortest plant.

Comparing masses

Look and write.

Use your hands to make a balance scale, to remind yourself what the balance scales tell you.

carrot

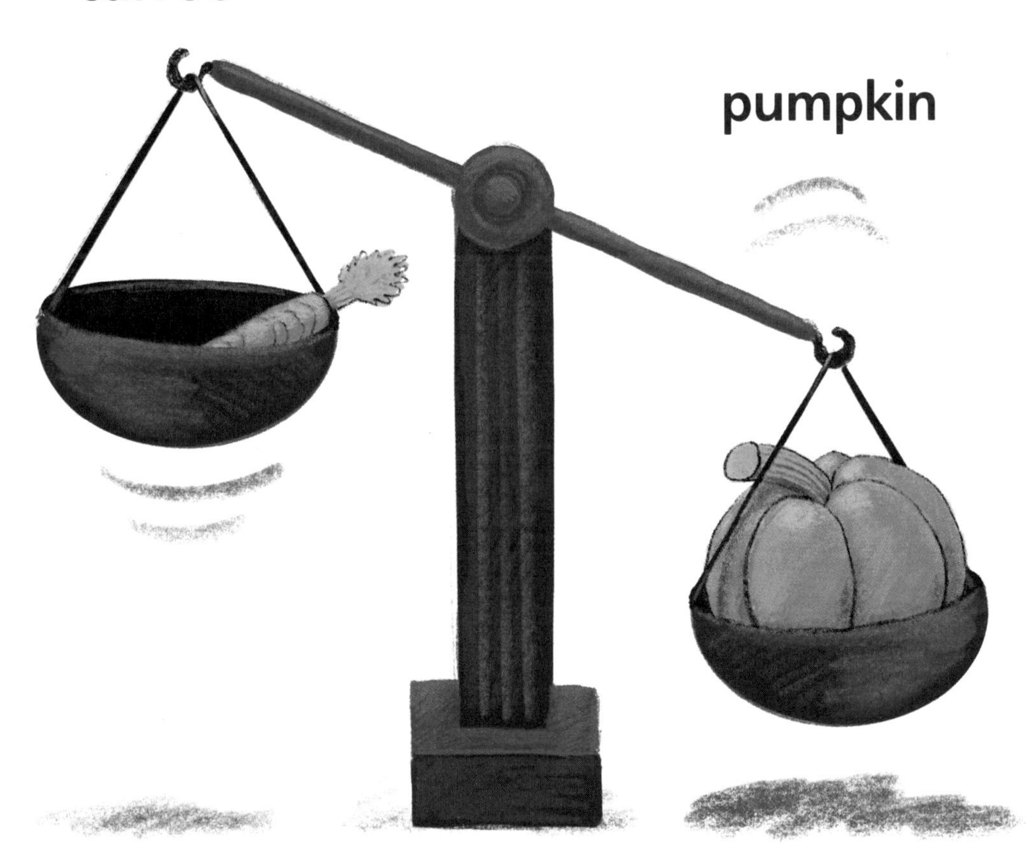

The ________________ is heavier than the ________________.

The ________________ is lighter than the ________________.

For practitioners

If children find the writing too difficult, they can draw the items in the spaces. Challenge them to draw a carrot and a pumpkin in the correct places on a mass arrow (see the Teacher's Resource) and to suggest a fruit or vegetable which might belong in the middle of the mass arrow.

Comparing capacities

Mark and say.

Tick the container in the first column that holds the most.

Circle the container in the first column that holds the least.

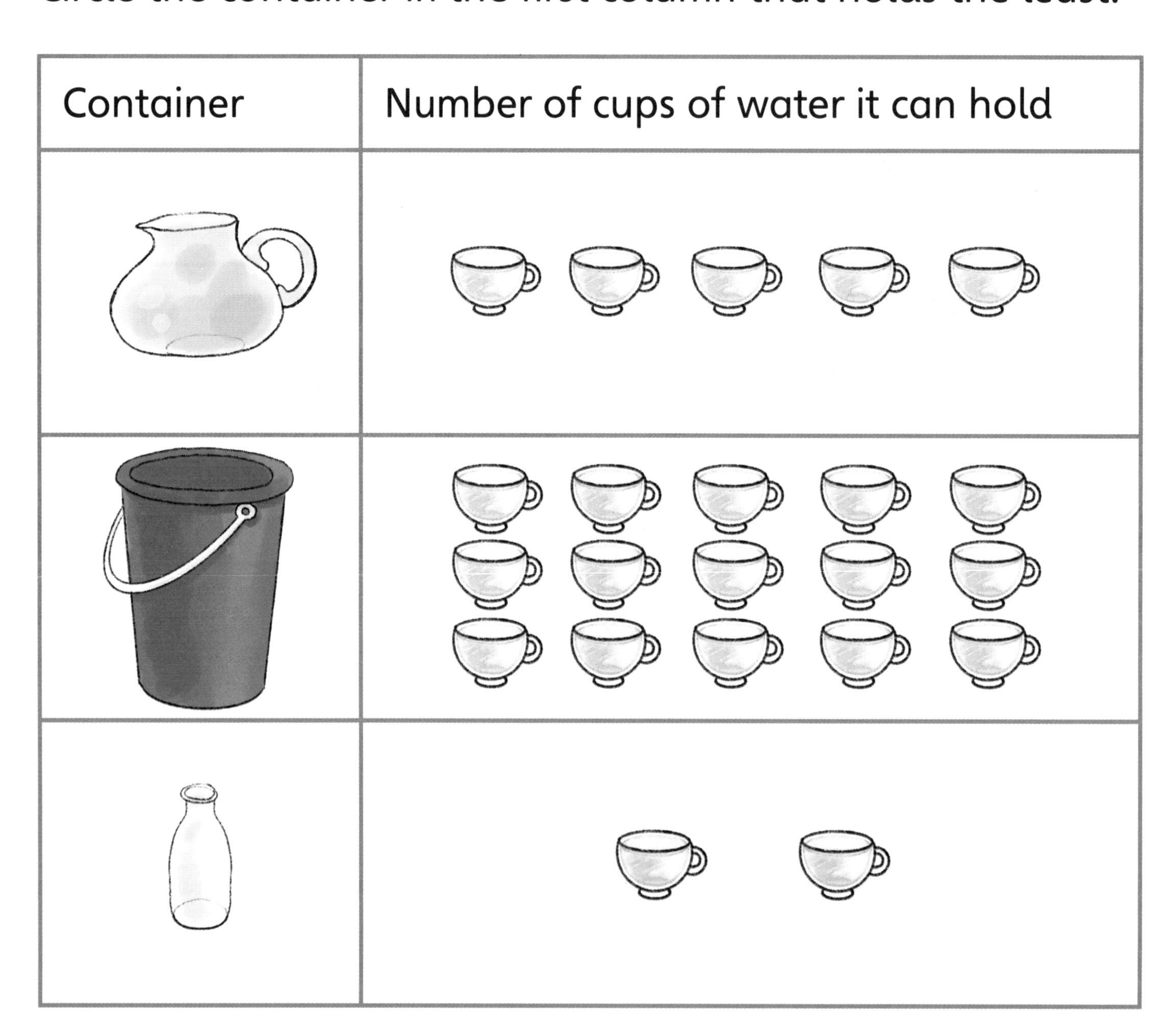

Container	Number of cups of water it can hold

For practitioners

The table shows the number of cups of water that each container can hold. Children could also draw the containers on a capacity arrow.

How many?

Count and write.

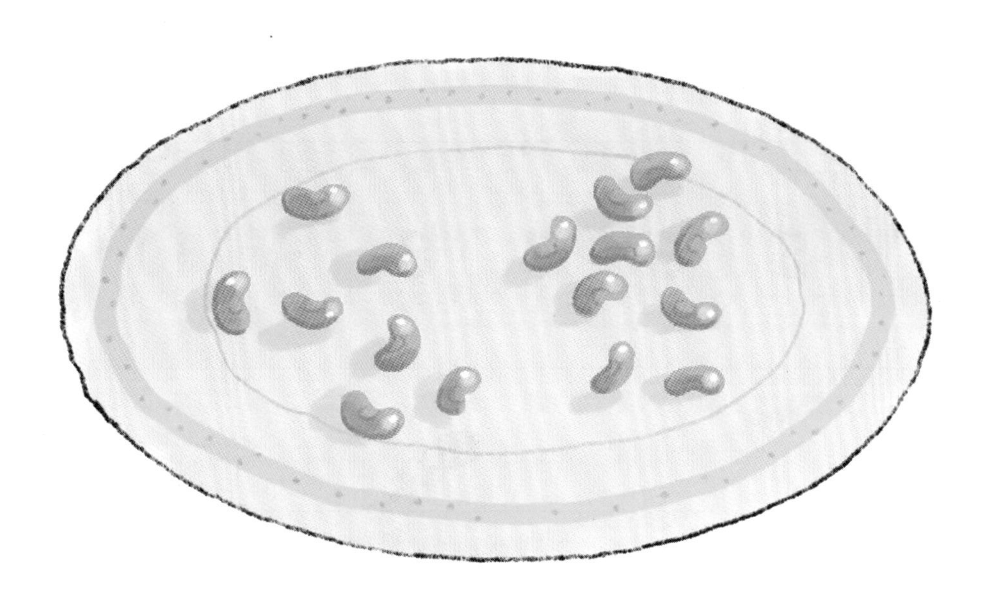

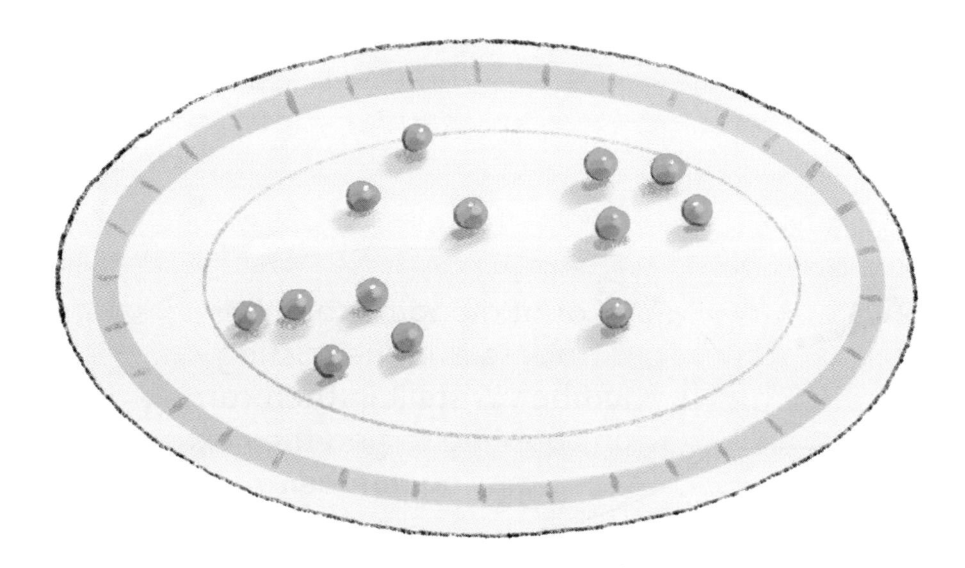

1	2	3	4	5	6	7	8	9	10	11	12	13	14	15	16	17	18	19	20

Which numbers are missing?

Write.

Write the missing numbers in the number track.

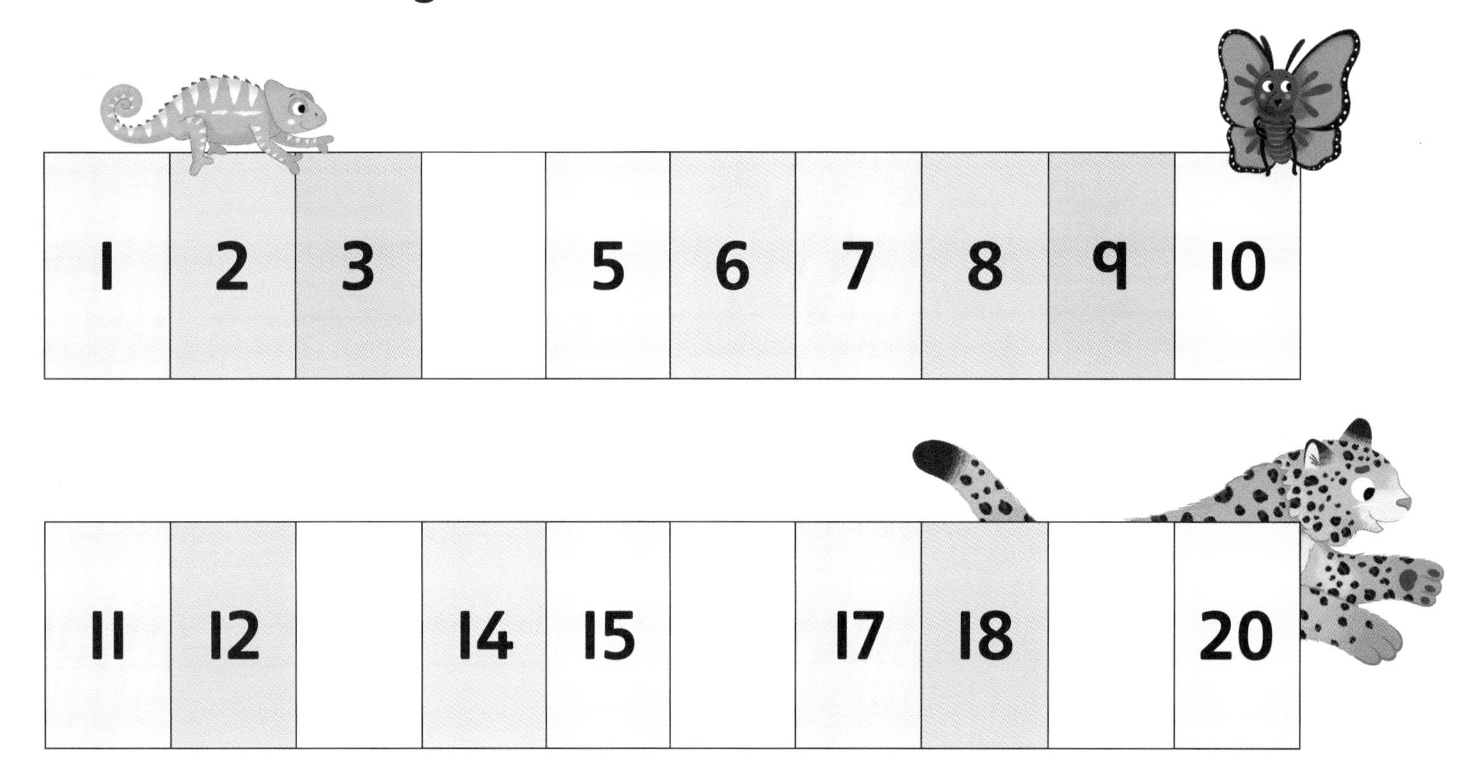

For practitioners

Encourage children to count along the number track to find the missing numbers. Challenge them to make their own number track.

Dot-to-dot

Join the dots.

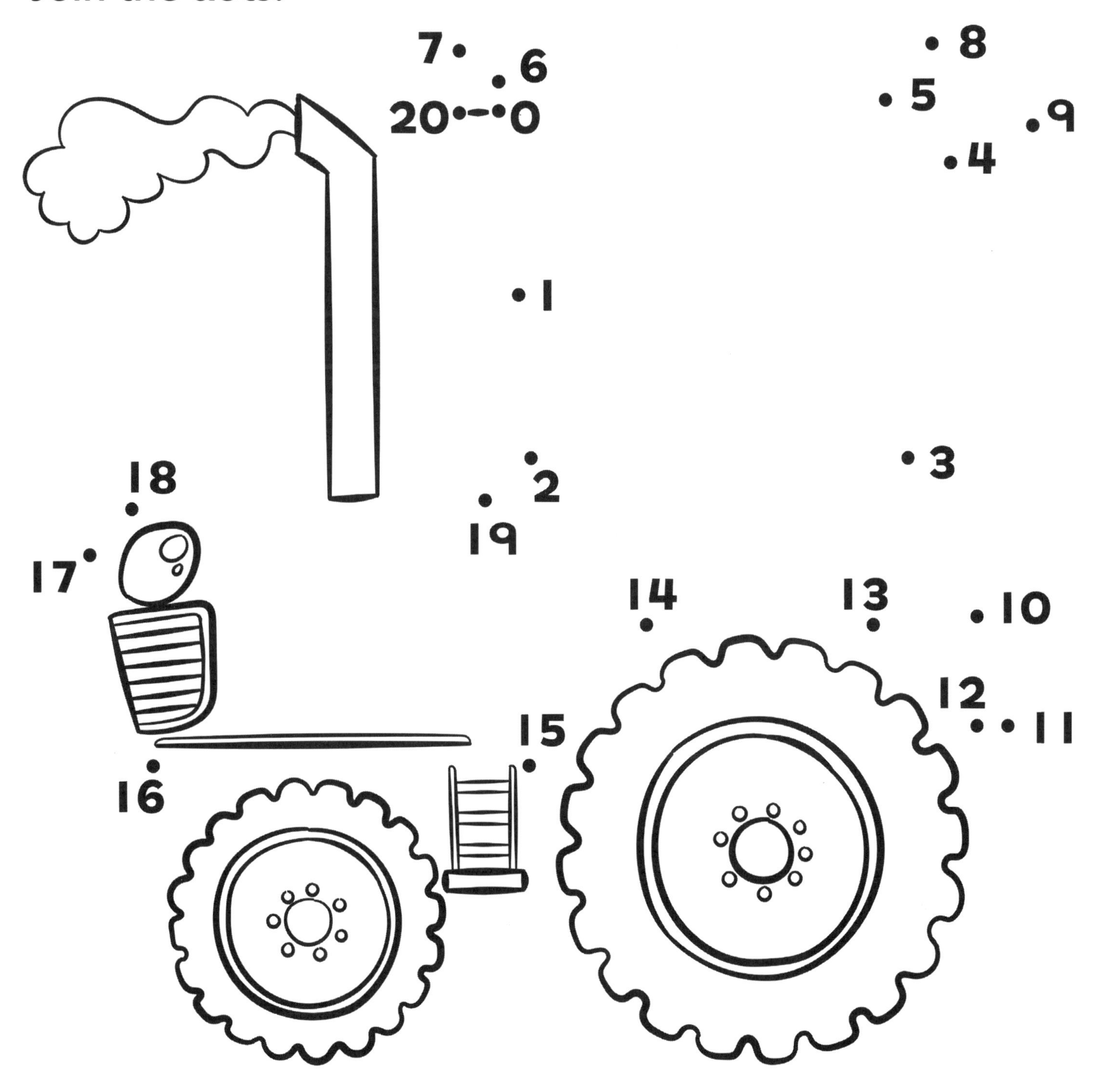

For practitioners

Encourage children to count from 0 to 20 to identify which dot to join to next.
Challenge them to make their own dot-to-dot, using thin paper over a simple picture to help them.

How much?

Draw and say.

Draw the coins you need to pay.

For practitioners

Give children a selection of coins to explore making the given amount before drawing the matching coins.

Stock your shop!

Draw and write.

Draw items in your shop and write their prices.

Item 1

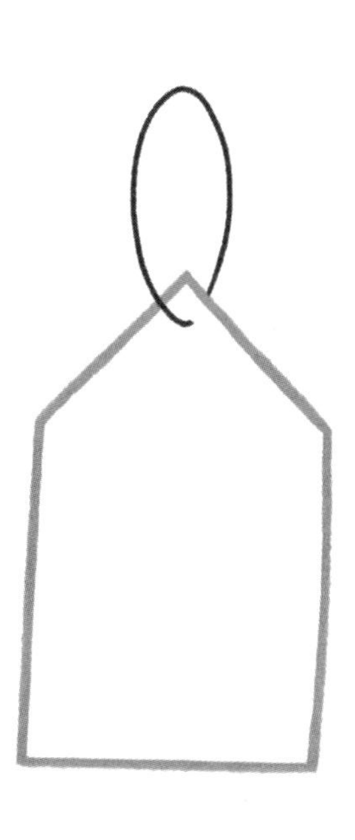

Item 2

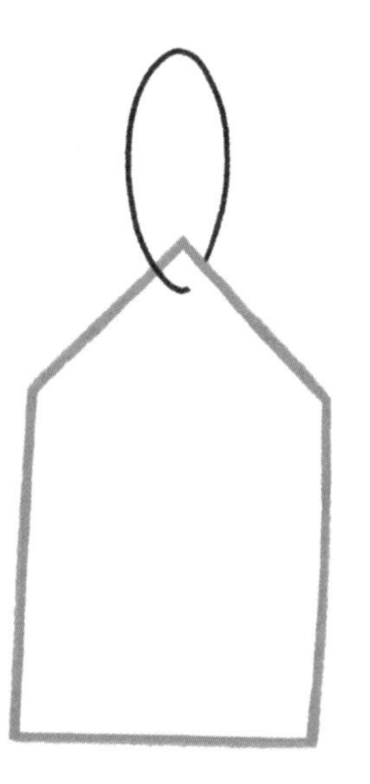

Item 3

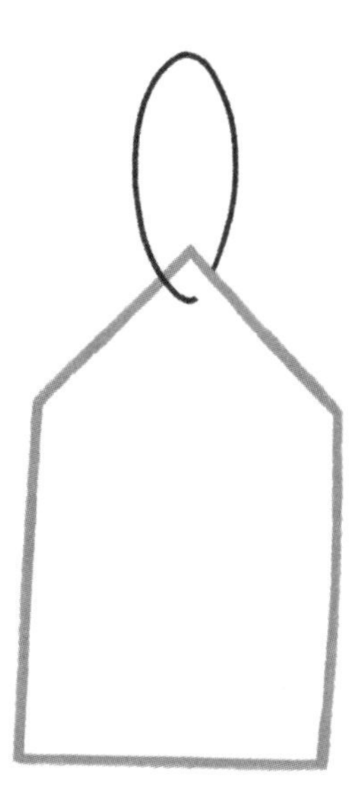

For practitioners

Children draw items for their shop and write their prices on the price tags. An item has been completed as an example. Give children a selection of coins to explore making a price before writing the amount. Challenge children to make a price with 3 or 4 coins.

Ordering by length

Look and tick.

Tick the fourth longest worm.

Cross out the seventh longest worm.

For practitioners

The worms are ordered by length. Children need to identify which worms are fourth and seventh in order of increasing length. Challenge children to measure some or all of the worms with paperclips.

Measure with cubes

Measure and write.

You will need some cubes.

Measure these pictures and write their length in cubes.

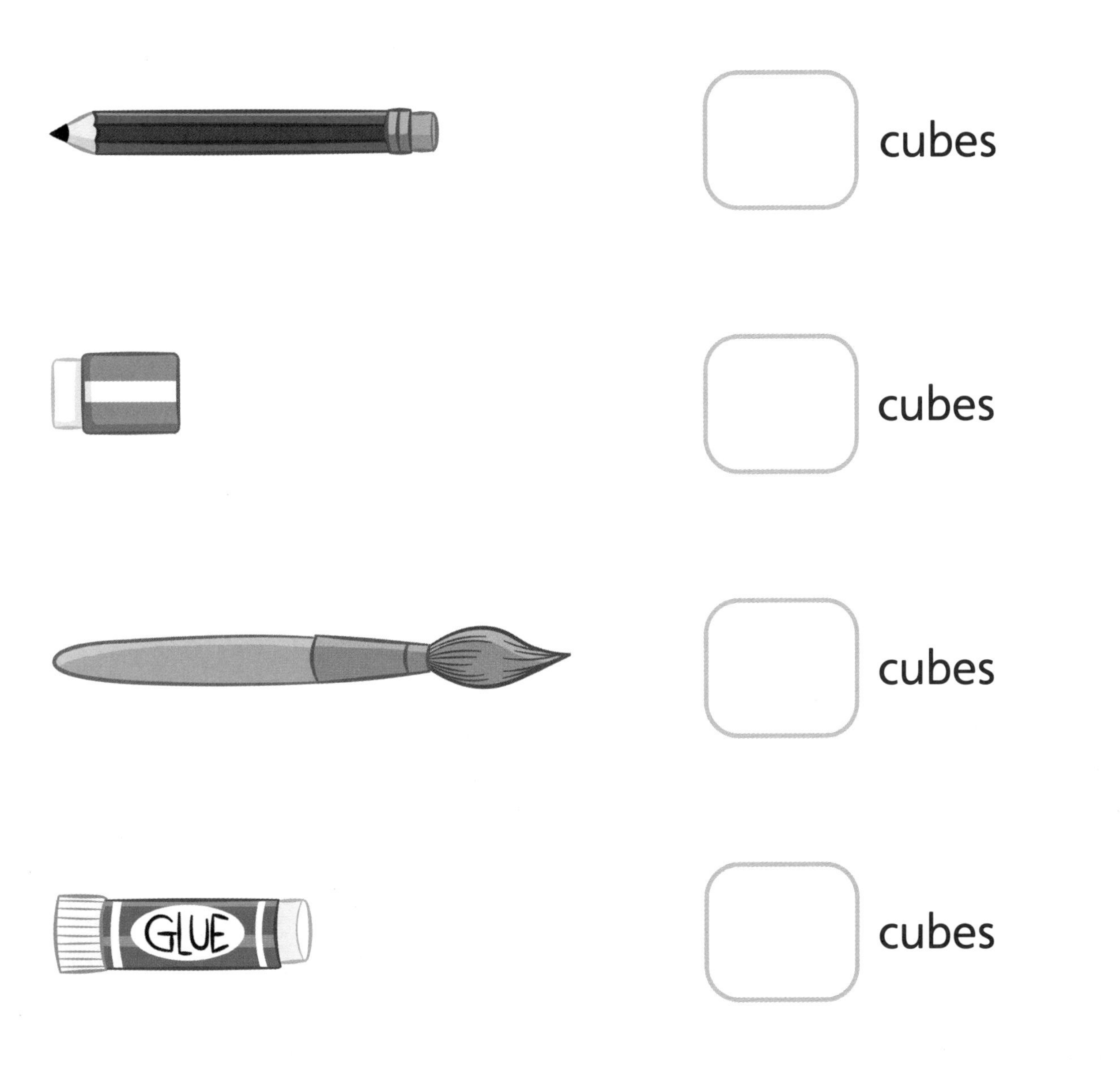

For practitioners

Children will need a set of cubes of the same size to measure with. Help them to measure and record the length of each pictured object. Challenge children to find the same objects in the classroom and measure them. Are any of the objects the same size as their picture?

Measuring

Measure and write.

Choose an object to measure with.
Measure how long the vegetables are.
Include the leaves and roots.

Do not leave any spaces when measuring with your object.

Draw the object you used
to measure.
For practitioners
Children can use cubes, paperclips, erasers, coins, etc., to measure the vegetables.
Children write the measurements in the boxes next to the vegetables.

Using a measuring strip

Measure and write.

Cut out the measuring strips.
Measure each object with
both measuring strips.

Line up the beginning of the measuring strip with one end of the object. Read and record the number closest to the other end of the object.

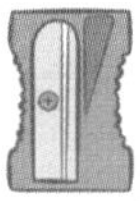

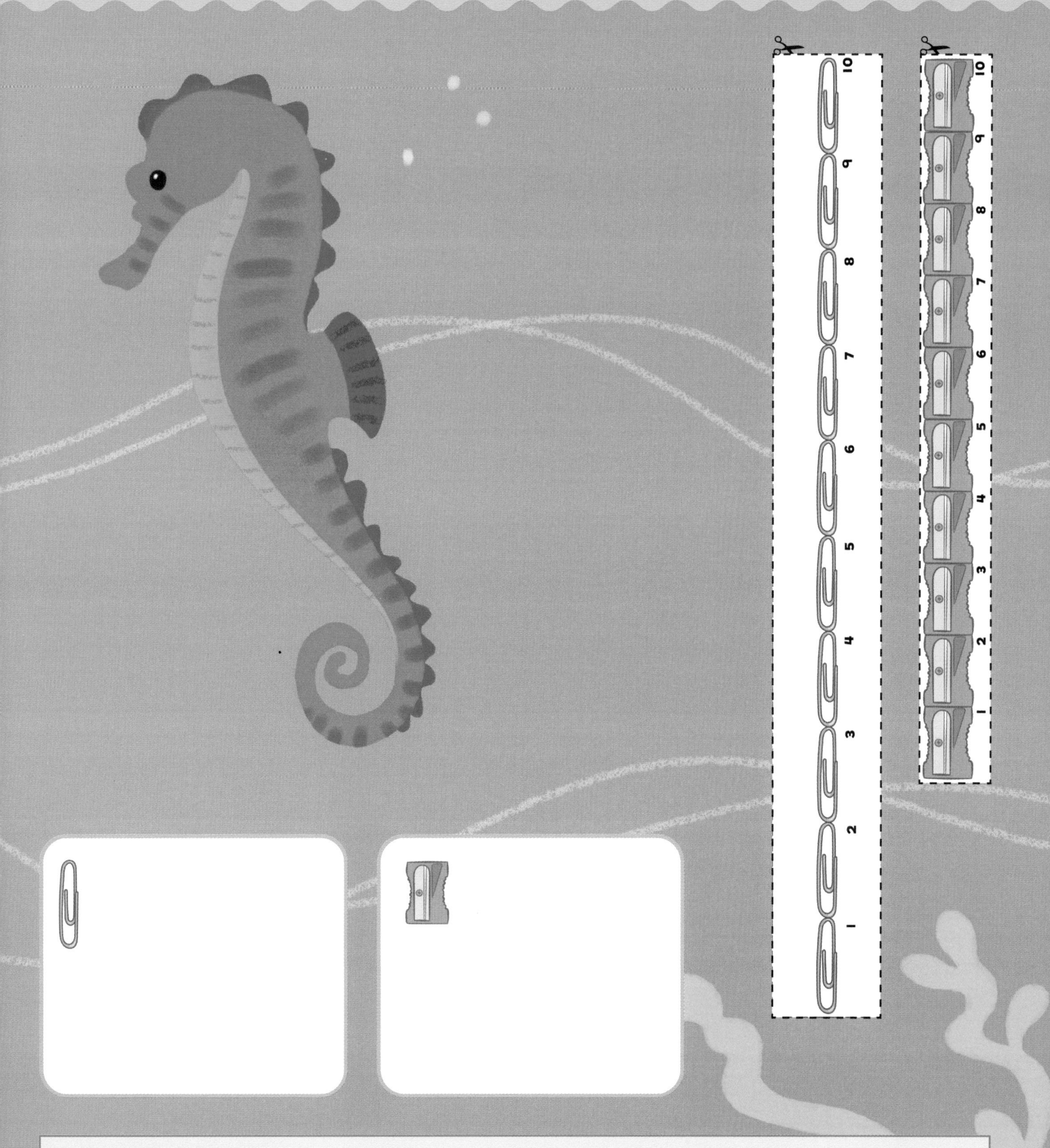

For practitioners

Cut out the 2 measuring strips. Support children to use the measuring strips correctly. Some may find it easier to measure both animals with 1 measuring strip first, then repeat with the other measuring strip. Ask children *How many paperclips did you need to measure the fish? How many pencil sharpeners? Why do you think there is a difference?*